TRUSTING GOD THROUGH

DIFFICULT
TIMES

A BIBLICAL REVIEW ON
THE LIFE OF JOSEPH

HAMP LEE III

(com)mission™

PUBLISHING

All scripture references used in this book are from the World
English Bible.

Cover photo courtesy of Andrei Cosma.

Trusting God Through Difficult Times/Hamp Lee III --
2nd edition.
ISBN 978-1-940042-28-2

TABLE OF CONTENTS

INTRODUCTION

Difficult times are like seasons. As summer and winter come and go, so do difficult times. But unlike the disappearing snow or warm weather, if you're not mindful, difficult seasons can leave behind bitterness, anger, hatred, and unforgiveness.

These emotions have the potential to negatively impact how you think, feel, and interact with everyone around you. But there's a way you can learn how to endure difficult seasons without allowing them to affect you in such a negative way.

Trusting God Through Difficult Times is a biblical review that follows the life of Joseph, a beloved son among twelve brothers. As his father's love for him spurred hatred in his brothers, Joseph found himself at the cusp of a thirteen-year ordeal filled with hardship and affliction. In spite of everything he faced, Joseph overcame his circumstances while serving as an inspiring example for anyone wanting to successfully endure difficult seasons of life.

The structure and format of *Trusting God Through Difficult Times* are a bit different from other biblical reviews. Every aspect of Joseph's life from Genesis 37 and Genesis 39-50 will not be outlined. This book will only capture the set of emotions and actions of those who acted against Joseph, his responses to those acts, and outline ten ways you can endure and overcome difficult seasons as a faithful man or woman of God. Therefore, I highly encourage you to read Genesis 37 and Genesis 39–50 before reading the first chapter.

1

OUTSIDE INFLUENCES

Difficult times often come through the actions of others, sometimes those closest to you. Pride might cause an individual to use his or her position or authority to exercise undue influence. Personal agendas drive some to selfishly coerce group decisions. Unfiltered anger might cause another to commit a heinous act such as physical assault. Such emotions and actions often derive from past internal conflicts that were never appropriately addressed or resolved. These individuals might have been hurt through some unrelated past event, and through their hurt, they in turn, hurt others.

Throughout this chapter, several individuals will be identified from Genesis 37 and Genesis 39-50 whose emotions and actions drove them to act against Joseph. There might be a few references on Joseph's responses to these acts in this chapter, but his responses will be detailed in the next chapter, Inward Responses.

As you read this chapter, consider whether you or someone you know has experienced similar emotions and mistreated others as a result.

Hatred and Envy

Jacob loved Joseph above his other sons, which Joseph's brothers envied and resented. Because of his great love for Joseph, Jacob made him a coat of many colors. When his brothers saw this, their hatred grew.

One day, Joseph had two dreams which he shared with his brothers and father. He described how in the first dream, his brothers had bowed down to him as sheaves in the field. His dream increased their hatred for him. In Joseph's second dream, his parents and brothers bowed down to him. This time, his father rebuked him, and the dream stirred envy within his brothers.[1]

Sometime later, Joseph's father wanted Joseph to check on his brothers and flocks in Shechem, about fifty miles north. Joseph travelled to

Shechem, but learned his brothers were in Dothan, another fifteen miles away.[2] As Joseph came toward them, they conspired to kill him and cast him in a pit:

"Come now therefore, and let's kill him, and cast him into one of the pits, and we will say, 'An evil animal has devoured him.' We will see what will become of his dreams."[3]

Reuben, the eldest brother, convinced the others to go forward with the plan except without killing Joseph. He hoped to deliver him back to his father later. When Joseph reached them, they stripped him of his coat and cast him into an empty pit. While the brothers sat down to eat, and Reuben was away, they conspired a new plan against Joseph.

As they watched a band of Midianite merchants traveling from Gilead to Egypt with camels carrying spicery, balm, and myrrh,[4] the fourth-eldest brother, Judah, said, "What profit is it if we kill our brother and conceal his blood? Come, and let's sell him to the Ishmaelites, and not let our hand be on him; for he is our brother, our flesh."[5]

The brothers took Joseph from the pit and sold him to the Midianites for twenty shekels of silver. When Reuben returned and found that Joseph wasn't in the pit, he tore his clothes as a sign of lament and distress. He came to his brothers and said, "The child is no more; and I, where will I go?"[6]

Deceit

The brothers then devised a plan to deceive their father. They wanted him to believe Joseph had been devoured by a beast. So they took Joseph's coat and dipped it in the blood of a goat they had killed. They brought the coat to their father and asked him to tell whether it was Joseph's.[7]

After Jacob acknowledged it was Joseph's coat, he did think that an evil beast had devoured him and that he had been torn to pieces. Jacob tore his clothes and put on sackcloth as a sign of mourning. He mourned for many days. And even though his sons and daughter came to comfort him, he refused to be comforted. Jacob was determined to die mourning for his son— and he wept for him.[8]

Even after seeing their father in distress, Joseph's brothers didn't come forward with the truth. For twenty-two years, they allowed their father to believe Joseph was dead.

Rejection

After traveling with the Midianites for almost three hundred miles to Egypt, Joseph was sold to Potiphar, an officer of Pharaoh and captain of the guard. He was brought into Potiphar's house as a servant.

As Joseph was a handsome man, he soon caught the attention of Potiphar's wife. One day, she approached him for sex.[9] He refused and said, "Behold, my master doesn't know what is with me in the house, and he has put all that he has into my hand. No one is greater in this house than I am, and he has not kept back anything from me but you, because you are his wife. How then can I do this great wickedness, and sin against God?"[10]

Unfortunately Joseph's refusal did nothing to sway the desires of Potiphar's wife. Day after day she spoke to Joseph, but he would not listen to her, lie next to her, or even be with her.

One day when Joseph was conducting his business alone in the house, Potiphar's wife caught him by his garment and urged him to have sex with her. He quickly fled from her presence, leaving his garment in her hand.[11] She called to the men of her house and said, "Behold, he has brought a Hebrew in to us to mock us. He came in to me to lie with me, and I cried with a loud voice. When he heard that I lifted up my voice and cried, he left his garment by me, and ran outside."[12]

She kept Joseph's garment with her until Potiphar returned home. When he arrived, she repeated her story. Potiphar became so angry that he took Joseph and placed him in the prison where the king held his prisoners.[13]

Joseph had gone from a beloved son to a slave and now a prisoner.

2

INWARD RESPONSES

During Joseph's thirteen years of hardship and affliction in Potiphar's house and in prison, a few of his responses were recorded.

Egypt

After being sold into slavery by his own brothers, and again by the Midianites, there is no mention of Joseph acting in a rebellious manner while in captivity. He served Potiphar in such a manner that Potiphar recognized that the Lord was with Joseph and how the Lord made everything he did to prosper. Joseph found grace in the sight of Potiphar and was made an overseer of his house and all that he had. Joseph served Potiphar, and the Lord blessed his home for Joseph's sake. Potiphar's trust in Joseph was so great that outside of the bread he ate, Potiphar didn't know what he had.[14]

Potiphar's Wife

Behold, my master doesn't know what is with me in the house, and he has put all that he has into my hand. No one is greater in this house than I am, and he has not kept back anything from me but you, because you are his wife. How then can I do this great wickedness, and sin against God? [15]

Throughout Joseph's ordeal with Potiphar's wife, he displayed great integrity and commitment not only to Potiphar as his servant, but also to God. He referred to adultery as a great wickedness, where he would sin against God. However, Potiphar's wife used her confrontation with Joseph to falsely accuse him of attempted rape. When Potiphar had heard of this, he put Joseph in prison.

Prison

After being sold into slavery twice and placed in prison for a crime he hadn't committed, the Lord continued to be with Joseph. The Lord showed him mercy and gave him favor with the prison keeper. As with Potiphar, the prison keeper committed everything in his control to Joseph.[16] He trusted Joseph so much that he didn't track his work, and everything Joseph did, the Lord made to prosper.[17]

Trusting God

Sometime later, both the chief of the butlers and the chief of the bakers offended Pharaoh, the king of Egypt, and he became angry with them. He placed them in the house of Potiphar, into the prison where Joseph was kept. Potiphar charged Joseph to be with them, and he served them as long as they remained in custody.

One night, both the chief butler and the chief baker each had a dream.[18] When Joseph saw them the next morning, he took notice of their countenances and asked why they looked sad. When they said they were sad because there was no interpreter for their dreams, Joseph said to them, "Don't interpretations belong to God? Please tell it to me."[19]

After being sold into slavery twice, falsely accused of a crime he hadn't committed, and placed in prison, Joseph's trust in God didn't waver. He trusted God to provide an interpretation of their dreams.

In the butler's dream, a vine was in front of him. It had three branches that budded and had blossoms that brought forth clusters of ripe grapes. As Pharaoh's cup was in his hand, he pressed the grapes from the vine into Pharaoh's cup and presented it into Pharaoh's hand.[20]

After hearing the dream, Joseph told the butler that the three branches represented three days. Within those days, Pharaoh would lift up his head and restore him as the chief butler, as he had been before. Joseph asked, when his position was restored, to remember him, show him kindness, and have him released from the prison. Joseph explained that he had been stolen away from the land of the Hebrews and had done nothing deserving of his placement in the dungeon.[21]

When the chief baker heard the positive interpretation, he shared his dream. In it, he had three white baskets stacked on his head. In the top basket, there were all types of baked goods, and birds ate them out of the basket. Joseph told the baker that the three baskets on his head represented three days. Within those days, Pharaoh would lift his head from his body, and birds would eat his flesh off him.

Three days later, Pharaoh held a birthday feast for all his servants. He lifted up the heads of the chief butler and chief baker. As Joseph had interpreted, the chief butler was restored to his position, and the chief baker was hanged. However, the chief butler didn't remember Joseph for two years.[22]

Pharaoh

Two years later, Pharaoh had two dreams in one night, and his spirit was troubled because of them. He called for all the magicians and wise men of Egypt to interpret his dreams, but there was no one among them who could.[24]

The chief butler then remembered his offense of forgetting Joseph in prison. He spoke to Pharaoh on how Joseph had accurately interpreted his and the chief baker's dreams. Pharaoh had Joseph quickly brought out of the prison. When he had shaved and received a change of clothes, Joseph was presented before Pharaoh.

Pharaoh told Joseph he had a dream that no one could interpret but heard he could. Joseph replied that it was not in him but God who would give him an answer of peace.[24]

Pharaoh then shared his dreams with Joseph. In the first dream, he was standing on the banks of the Nile River when seven plump and attractive cows came up out of the river and fed on the reed grass. Seven other cows came up after them, and they were poor, very ugly, and thin. He had never seen such cows in all of Egypt.

The seven poor, ugly, and thin cows ate the seven plump cows, but no one would have been able to tell they had done so, because they were just as poor, ugly, and thin as before.

In Pharaoh's second dream, he saw seven ears of corn growing on one stalk, full and good. Then he saw another seven ears sprouting up, but they were thin and blasted by the east wind. The thin ears swallowed up the seven good ears.

Joseph said that Pharaoh's dreams were one and the same, and that God had revealed to him what He was about to do. The seven good cows and ears represented seven years of plenty, and the seven poor, ugly, and thin cows and seven empty ears represented seven years of famine. Joseph said there would be seven years of great plenty in Egypt, and afterward would come seven years of famine. The famine would be so severe that the seven years of plenty would be forgotten in the land.[25] And because the dream had been doubled, Joseph said that God would shortly bring it to pass.

Joseph suggested to Pharaoh that he search for a discreet and wise man to set over Egypt. This man would appoint officers over the land and take up a fifth part of the land throughout the seven plenteous years. The food would be kept in the cities to ensure that the people of the land wouldn't perish during the years of famine.

Pharaoh and all his servants were pleased with Joseph's recommendation. He acknowledged that in all that God had shown Joseph, there was no one as discreet and wise as him. Pharaoh said to his servants, "Can we find such a one as this, a man in whom is the Spirit of God?"

Pharaoh then placed Joseph over his house, and according to Joseph's word would all of Pharaoh's people be ruled. Pharaoh would only be greater than Joseph in regard to the throne. Pharaoh said to Joseph, "See, I have set you over all the land of Egypt."[26]

After being sold into slavery twice, God was with Joseph, and Potiphar placed him over all of his house. After being falsely accused of attempted rape and placed in prison, God was with Joseph, and the prison keeper placed him over the prison. And after thirteen years of hardship and affliction in Egypt, Pharaoh recognized the Spirit of God in Joseph and placed him over the entire land.

Pharaoh gave Joseph his signet ring, along with clothing of fine linen and a gold chain. Joseph rode in the second chariot, and they called out before him, "Bow the knee!" Pharaoh also gave him the name Zaphenath-paneah, as well as the priest of On's daughter as his wife.

Joseph woke up that morning a prisoner and went to bed as a ruler over Egypt...with a wife.

Leading a Nation

At thirty years of age, Joseph was now a ruler over Egypt and set out to complete his work.[27] During the seven plenteous years, Joseph diligently gathered food by the handful. He stored food in the cities and fields across Egypt. Joseph gathered so much corn that it was as numerous as the sand of the sea.

Before the years of famine came, Joseph and his wife had two sons. Their firstborn was named Manasseh, for Joseph said that God made him forget all of his toil and his father's house. His second son was named Ephraim, for God caused him to be fruitful in the land of his affliction.[28]

When the seven years of famine finally came, there was famine across all lands, but there was bread in Egypt. When the people of Egypt became famished themselves, they cried out to Pharaoh for bread. Pharaoh told them to go to Joseph and do whatever he said. As they came to Joseph, he opened the storehouses and sold food to them. Joseph had gathered so much food that Egypt could support its own people and all the earth.

Family Reunion

When Jacob learned there was corn in Egypt, he sent ten of his sons to purchase some.[29] However, Jacob didn't send his youngest son,

Benjamin, because he feared something bad might happen to him.[30]

When Joseph's brothers came before him, they bowed down with their faces to the earth. Joseph recognized his brothers, but they didn't recognize him.[31] Joseph remembered his dreams from years prior.[32] Joseph then treated them like strangers and spoke roughly to them.

In their dialogue, Joseph accused them of being spies to see the nakedness of the land, but they denied his accusations. They said they were of twelve brothers; one was with their father, and the other was dead. Joseph told them that in order for them to prove they were not spies, they had to stay in Egypt unless their youngest brother joined them.

Joseph said that one of them could go fetch their brother, but the others would be kept in prison to prove whether there was any truth in them. Instead, he placed them all in prison for three days. [33]

On the third day, Joseph told them to do what he said because he feared God. He said that he would keep one in prison while the others delivered corn to their homes, asking them to return with their youngest brother so that their words would be proven and not die.[34]

Among themselves they said, "We are certainly guilty concerning our brother, in that we saw the distress of his soul, when he begged us, and we wouldn't listen. Therefore this distress has come upon us." Reuben answered them, saying, "Didn't I tell you, saying, 'Don't sin against the child,' and you wouldn't listen? Therefore also, behold, his blood is required."

After twenty-two years, they continued to carry the guilt of what they had done to Joseph. They thought this was the reason for the distress coming upon them. However, what the brothers didn't know was that Joseph could understand them. He had been using an interpreter to speak to them. Joseph then turned away from them and cried. Once he returned, he spoke to them further and took their brother Simeon, binding him before their eyes.[35]

Before they departed, Joseph commanded that their sacks be filled with corn and each man's money be returned to his sack. He also gave them provisions for their return journey home.

Though his brothers had stripped him of his coat of many colors, thrown him in a pit, and sold him to the Midianites for twenty shekels of silver twenty-two years earlier, he harbored no ill toward them. This is extremely important to understand. Had he allowed any bitterness, unforgiveness, hatred, and so on to rule within his heart, it might have affected his rule over Egypt and his dealings with his brothers. Joseph might have sought to avenge the years of hardship and affliction he had experienced rather than cry and show kindness toward them by giving them free corn and provisions for their journey home.

A Truth Revealed

After the brothers returned to Egypt with Benjamin and were ready to go back home again, Joseph commanded the steward of his house to fill their sacks with as much food as they could carry. He again had each of the brothers' money returned into the top of their sacks, including the money they had tried to return from their first visit. Joseph also had his silver cup placed at the top of Benjamin's sack.

When the men had gone a short distance from the city, Joseph instructed his steward to go after them saying, "Why have you rewarded evil for good? Isn't this that from which my lord drinks, and by which he indeed divines? You have done evil in so doing."[36]

The brothers denied the accusation and even mentioned how they had returned the money they had found in their sacks from their first visit to Egypt. So how then could they steal silver or gold from his master's house? They said, "With whomever of your servants it is found, let him die, and we also will be my lord's slaves."[37] But the steward replied that whomever the cup was found with would become his servant, and the rest would be innocent.

The brothers quickly lowered their sacks to the ground and opened them. The steward began his search with the eldest brother until he reached the youngest. When the cup was found in Benjamin's sack, the brothers tore their clothes as a sign of distress, loaded their donkeys, and returned back to Egypt.

When they arrived at Joseph's house, they fell before him. Joseph asked why they did this and whether they knew someone like him who practiced divination. Judah asked what could they say to clear themselves. God had found out their guilt and committed them all as Joseph's servants; however, Joseph replied that only Benjamin would be his servant, and the rest could return to their father in peace.

Judah went up to him again and asked if he could speak once more and not have Joseph become angry with him, as Joseph was like Pharaoh himself. Judah explained how Joseph had asked about their father and youngest brother and asked to see the brother.[38] He had said to Joseph previously, "We said to my lord, 'The boy can't leave his father, for if he should leave his father, his father would die.' You said to your servants, 'Unless your youngest brother comes down with you, you will see my face no more.' When we came up to your servant my father, we told him the words of my lord. Our father said, 'Go again and buy us a little food.' We said, 'We can't go down. If our youngest brother is with us, then we will go down: for we may not see the man's face, unless our youngest brother is with us.' Your servant, my father, said to us, 'You know that my wife bore me two sons. One went out from me, and I said, "Surely he is torn in pieces;" and I haven't seen him since. If you take this one also from me, and harm happens to him, you will bring down my gray hairs with sorrow to Sheol.'"[39]

Judah spoke for the brothers again: "Now therefore when I come to your servant my father, and the boy is not with us; since his life is bound up in the boy's life; it will happen, when he sees that the boy is no more, that he will die. Your servants will bring down the gray hairs of your servant, our father, with sorrow to Sheol."[40]

Judah said that he had become collateral for his youngest brother. If he didn't return him, he would bear the blame all of his life. Judah asked Joseph if he could remain in place of his brother as his servant and allow Benjamin to return home. Judah feared to see the evil that would find his father.

After hearing this, Joseph couldn't contain himself any longer. He had everyone leave his presence except his brothers. He wept so loudly that the Egyptians and the household of Pharaoh heard him.

He then said to his brothers, "I am Joseph! Does my father still live?"[41]

His brothers were speechless. They were troubled at his presence. The last time they had seen Joseph was after selling him into slavery twenty-two years earlier. Now, he stood before them as a ruler of Egypt.

Joseph asked them to come closer to him. When they did, he told them that he was their brother whom they sold into Egypt. However, he didn't want them to feel distressed or angry with themselves for selling him. God had sent him before them to preserve their lives.

Joseph told them to quickly return to their father and let him know that he was alive and was lord of all Egypt, and to come down without delay. Joseph would bring them to the land of Goshen to live so they would be close to him. He told them that he would nourish them, as there were five years of famine remaining.

After reiterating his message, he fell on Benjamin's neck and cried. Benjamin then cried on his neck. He also kissed each of his brothers, cried upon them, and continued speaking with them.

Jacob's Death

Seventeen years later, Joseph and his brothers buried their father in the land of Canaan and returned to Egypt. His brothers thought Joseph would hate them and would avenge all the evil they had done to him. So they sought to deceive him by sending a message to Joseph saying their father had given a command before he died: "Now please forgive the disobedience of your brothers, and their sin, because they did evil to you. Now, please forgive the disobedience of the servants of the God of your father."[42]

Joseph cried when he heard the message. His brothers then came in, fell down before him, and declared they were his servants. But Joseph reiterated his previous response when he had revealed himself to them: "Don't be afraid, for am I in the place of God? As for you, you meant evil against me, but God meant it for good, to save many people alive, as is happening today. Now therefore don't be afraid. I will provide for you and your little ones." Joseph then comforted his brothers and spoke kindly to them.[43]

Thirty-nine years had passed since his brothers had sold him into slavery. However, they continued to hold onto the fear of Joseph avenging himself, even though he had told them seventeen years earlier not to be angry with themselves for selling him, because it was God that had sent him before them to preserve life.[44]

For Further Study

Though I've reviewed specific portions of Joseph's hardship and affliction, several others in Genesis 37 and Genesis 39-50 also experienced difficult seasons. Please review these scriptures and describe the difficulties each person (or group) experienced, any assistance they received, and the outcome of their circumstances:

Joseph's Brothers

Jacob

Pharaoh

3

YOUR RESPONSE

The difficult seasons you experience can have a positive or negative impact on your life and those around you. If you're able to respond to difficult times as Joseph had, you'll have an opportunity to live in godliness, accomplish God's will, and see many blessings come to you and others. However, if you harbor bitterness, anger, or unforgiveness, you'll have a difficult time trusting people and seeing the good in others. You'll keep yourself chained to the memory of an event, though years and decades might pass by. You'll do nothing but spoil everyone and everything around you, affecting your ability to serve God wholeheartedly.

So how should you respond to difficult times?

1. Stop repeating the injustice or difficult situation in your mind.

He who covers an offense promotes love; but he who repeats a matter separates best friends.[45]

Joseph didn't allow his injustice or captivity to dictate the direction of his thoughts, emotions, or heart. He didn't allow bitterness, anger, or revenge to control him. He remained faithful, compassionate, and wholly committed to God. And because of this, his perspective was open for God to shape and mold his character.

When you allow injustice or difficult situations to consume you, you're unable to think clearly or set your mind on godliness. Each time you repeat the issue in your mind, your heart grows darker, and you become less prone to forgive, show compassion, or obey God.[46] Your mind slowly becomes set on evil, disobedience, and sin.

However, if you're able to cover the offense and keep the injustice or situation from poisoning your mind and heart, you'll have the proper perspective to remain conscious of your mental state, temperament, and the purpose of your season.

2. Do not allow bitterness to take root.

Looking carefully lest there be any man who falls short of the grace of God, lest any root of bitterness springing up trouble you, and many be defiled by it... [47]

Bitterness is the root of trouble and evil desires. It ruins the beauty and innocence of pure hearts, good intentions, and godly actions. It springs up trouble in the form of hate, envy, selfishness, anger, unforgiveness, revenge, distrust, pain, and the like.[48]

As bitterness can poison your thoughts, words, and actions, you must pay close attention to the ebb and flow of your mind and heart. Be diligent, focused, and consistent so you don't fall short of the grace of God by allowing any root of bitterness to spring up in you.

3. Walk in forgiveness.

Bitterness breeds unforgiveness. It lives in the shadows of your mind, heart, and conscience. Unforgiveness warps your view of the world, the people around you, and the innocence of your heart. It chokes the life out of everything it touches, leaving an internal cycle of pain, suffering, and distrust. And if you choose to live under its control, it becomes a *poison* carrying eternal consequences:

For if you forgive men their trespasses, your heavenly Father will also forgive you. But if you don't forgive men their trespasses, neither will your Father forgive your trespasses.[49]

You do not forgive someone by accident. Forgiveness is an intentional and voluntary act where you change your feelings and attitude regarding an offense by letting go of negative emotions. Forgiveness is treating an offender as if he or she had never wronged you.

There might come a time when you want to forgive, but can't seem to get past the memories, emotions, and hurt committed against you. Maybe you don't want to forgive, even though you know you should. Either way, you feel chained to the injustice committed against you. And when this happens, it's important for you to ask God for His help and peace.

4. Allow God to search you and lead you.

Search me, God, and know my heart. Try me, and know my thoughts. See if there is any wicked way in me, and lead me in the everlasting way.[50]

When you notice the tides of difficult times beginning to affect you, allow God to search you, know your thoughts and heart, and try you. He'll expose the deepest issues stirring within you, lead you safely through any internal or external turmoil, and bring you into pastures of refreshing peace.[51] Now, His leading might not physically deliver you out of your difficult situation, but He will help you live righteously through seasons of injustice and adversity.

5. Live faithfully.

Without faith it is impossible to be well pleasing to him, for he who comes to God must believe that he exists, and that he is a rewarder of those who seek him.[52]

Hebrews 11:1 says that faith is assurance of the things hoped for and the proof of things not seen. Now, if you read through Hebrews 11, you'll read about people who faced significant trials and tribulations. The faith they displayed was rooted in their trust in God and the hope of an eternal existence beyond their circumstances (the assurance). The proof of what they hoped for was shown through their actions. They lived faithfully because they knew they would be rewarded for living a life that pleased God—not only through their difficult season, or some other challenge in life, but for all eternity.[53]

Live a life worthy of God's reward by placing your faith in Him. Keep your focus on what God has promised you through faith, not on earthly treasures or the thought of redemption, affirmation, or vindication from those who mistreat you. Please God through faithful service.

6. Do not harbor anger.

The discretion of a man makes him slow to anger. It is his glory to overlook an offense.[54]

When you feel wronged, you can become so emotional that you lose (or relinquish) self-control and act out in uncontrollable anger, affecting everyone around you. However, exercising discretion through understanding, prudence, and insight will allow you to slow your anger.[56] You'll be quick to listen, slow to speak, and slow to become angry. Then, you'll have an opportunity to see your situation from a godly perspective and exercise patience and godliness as you await God's wisdom, deliverance, and perfect will to manifest.

Additionally, it is to your glory (benefit, honor, and splendor) to overlook an offense. To overlook an offense is to intentionally move beyond it or step over it. An offense is not something you stop in front of, meditate on, or mull over. You walk away from it and don't turn back.

7. Do not envy sinners.

Don't fret because of evildoers, neither be envious against those who work unrighteousness. For they shall soon be cut down like the grass, and wither like the green herb. Trust in [the Lord], and do good. Dwell in the land, and enjoy safe pasture.[56]

There might come a time when you see those responsible for your injustice and suffering receive promotions, recognition, and wealth—sometimes at your expense. While you're facing trials and tribulations, you see them laughing and enjoying their lives without the slightest concern for what they've done to you. And seeing their success and enjoyment might make you not only bitter and angry but also envious of what they have.

When envy grows within you, so does selfishness, deviant behavior, and a lack of faith. Though you might think you want what these individuals have, there is a "price" and an expected end for sin:

For the wages of sin is death, but the free gift of God is eternal life in Christ Jesus our Lord.[57]

Though it might seem that evildoers succeed, the few years they spend in luxury on this earth will pale in comparison to their eternal condemnation.[58] As Psalm 37:2 says, they will soon be cut down like grass and wither.

Instead of having envious desires, you can pray for those who are persecuting you and to minister to them through your service. You might be the only Christian they know, and through your intercession and commitment to God, they might come to believe in Jesus and escape the eternal condemnation to come.

You have heard that it was said, 'You shall love your neighbor and hate your enemy.' But I tell you, love your enemies, bless those who curse you, do good to those who hate you, and pray for those who mistreat you and persecute you, that you may be children of your Father who is in heaven. For he makes his sun to rise on the evil and the good, and sends rain on the just and the unjust. For if you love those who love you, what reward do you have? Don't even the tax collectors do the same? If you only greet your friends, what more do you do than others? Don't even the tax collectors do the same? Therefore you shall be perfect, just as your Father in heaven is perfect.[59]

8. Live in humility.

Pride goes before destruction, and an arrogant spirit before a fall.[60]

In its most basic function, pride causes you to believe your position, thoughts, or actions are "right" and that everyone else is wrong. It blinds you from seeing the true condition of life and how your words and actions negatively impact everything and everyone around you. While you're trying not to seem weak or like a pushover, dreams die, relationships crumble, goals remain unmet, and people are left hurting and damaged. Pride keeps you from saying, "I love you. I'm sorry. I was wrong; forgive me. Can we start again?"

A man's pride brings him low, but one of lowly spirit gains honor.[61]

Humility is the quality or condition of a modest opinion or estimation of your own importance or rank. Humility can provide opportunities to restore relationships, seek forgiveness, and consider the needs of others above your own.[62] And when you exercise humility, God can use your life and works to bring glory to Himself, and maybe save nations of people because of it.[63]

9. Be still.

It isn't good to have zeal without knowledge, nor being hasty with one's feet and missing the way.[64]

When you're experiencing difficult times, you might want to end your injustice, suffering, and pain as soon as possible. You might believe that being still accomplishes nothing and that some movement in any direction is better than no movement at all. And though you believe some movement might get you closer to a peaceful state, you might find yourself further from God's will because you're moving when God wants you to remain still. This is why those who are hasty to move miss the way. They fail to consider God's path for their lives.

When you find yourself in the midst of a difficult season, it's important to remain still and patiently wait for God. Spend your time gaining godly knowledge. Serve faithfully. Strive to find your rest and peace in Him.

Rejoice in the Lord always! Again I will say, "Rejoice!" Let your gentleness be known to all men. The Lord is at hand. In nothing be anxious, but in everything, by prayer and petition with thanksgiving, let your requests be made known to God. And the peace of God, which surpasses all understanding, will guard your hearts and your thoughts in Christ Jesus.[65]

10. Allow patience to perfect you as you wait for God's deliverance.

Count it all joy, my brothers, when you fall into various temptations, knowing that the testing of your faith produces endurance. Let endurance have its perfect work, that you may be perfect and complete, lacking in nothing.

But if any of you lacks wisdom, let him ask of God, who gives to all liberally and without reproach, and it will be given to him. But let him ask in faith, without any doubting, for he who doubts is like a wave of the sea, driven by the wind and tossed. For that man shouldn't think that he will receive anything from the Lord. He is a double-minded man, unstable in all his ways.[66]

Considering various temptations (and difficult times) as a joy might seem like a strange endeavor. However, these situations are meant to be joyous because they provide the ideal environment for a person to grow as a man or woman of God. By allowing patience to have her perfect work in you, you'll learn how to work through your personal issues, live in godliness, and walk in obedience to God's will in spite of your circumstances. You'll be perfected as a man or woman of God, not wanting or lacking anything.

With the turmoil that comes through difficult times, you might not always know what to do or where to start. When you seem confused or unsure, ask God for wisdom. As you seek His wisdom, ask in faith. Wait patiently and trust Him to respond with an answer at the proper time. If you waver in doubt or unbelief, do not think you'll receive anything from God. You'll be double minded and unstable in *all* your ways.

CONCLUSION

As difficult times are woven into the seasons of your life, they have the potential to positively or negatively impact your perspective and how you interact with the world around you. Your response to difficulties might save generations of people, or it might send you and others along a dangerous path of destruction, pain, and sadness for many years to come.

With such significant opportunities or consequences, I pray *Trusting God Through Difficult Times* has helped you navigate through your difficult seasons of life. I pray you were able to see Joseph's integrity, compassion, and faithfulness in spite of the adversity he endured. I pray that his life encouraged you to persevere through yours.

God is not slack concerning His promises. Trust in Him. Live faithfully. Wait patiently for His deliverance.[67] Your faithfulness might be the catalyst for experiencing God's deliverance and the means by which many others will one day find safety, freedom, and belief in Jesus.

END NOTES

1—Genesis 37:3–11

2—Genesis 37:12–17

3—Genesis 37:20

4—Genesis 37:25

5—Genesis 37:26-27

6—Genesis 37:30

7—Genesis 37:31-32

8—Genesis 37:34-35

9—Genesis 39:7

10—Genesis 39:8-9

11—Genesis 39:11-12

12—Genesis 39:13-15

13—Genesis 39:19-20

14—Genesis 39:1-6

15—Genesis 39:8-9

16—Genesis 39:21-22

17—Genesis 39:23

18—Genesis 40:5

19—Genesis 40:8

20—Genesis 40:9-11

21—Genesis 40:12-15

22—Genesis 40:20-23

23—Genesis 41:1-8

24—Genesis 41:15-16

25—Genesis 41:30-31

26—Genesis 41:39-41

27—Genesis 41:46

28—Genesis 41:50-52

29—Genesis 42:1-2

30—Genesis 42:4

31—Genesis 42:8

32—Genesis 37:5-11

33—Genesis 42:15-16

34—Genesis 42:20

35—Genesis 42:24

36—Genesis 44:4-5

37—Genesis 44:7-9

38—Genesis 44:19-21

39—Genesis 44:23-29

40—Genesis 44:30-31

41—Genesis 45:3

42—Genesis 50:17

43—Genesis 50:19-21

44—Genesis 45:4-5

45—Proverbs 17:9

46—Ephesians 4:17-19

47—Hebrews 12:15

48—Matthew 15:18-20

49—Matthew 6:14-15

50—Psalm 139:23-24

51—Psalm 1; Isaiah 1:18; John 16:13–15

52—Hebrews 11:6

53—Hebrews 11:13-16

54—Proverbs 19:11

55—James 1:19-20

56—Psalm 37:1-3

57—Romans 6:23

58—Luke 16:19-31

59—Matthew 5:43-48

60—Proverbs 16:18

61—Proverbs 29:23

62—Philippians 2:3

63—Matthew 5:14-16

64—Proverbs 19:2

65—Philippians 4:4-7

66—James 1:2-8

67—Jeremiah 31:31–34; Romans 8:29; Philippians 1:6; Matthew 6:14-15; Hebrews 11; 2 Peter 3:9

(com)mission™

PUBLISHING

www.commissionpubs.com
info@commissionpubs.com

www.ingramcontent.com/pod-product-compliance
Lightning Source LLC
Chambersburg PA
CBHW071744020426
42331CB00008B/2172